Just Between Friends

ISBN 0-915720-67-1

10 9 8 7 6 5 4 3

A Special Gift
For:

Margaret Miller

From:

Pat Crump

1 / 1991

God bless you,
   God bless our friendship —
            I love you,
                Pat

Love is blind;
friendship closes its eyes

— A FRENCH PROVERB

Just Between Friends

Written and Compiled by
MARY HOLLINGSWORTH

BROWNLOW PUBLISHING COMPANY
FORT WORTH, TEXAS

Other Brownlow Gift Books

*To each of you
whose special friendship has touched
and changed my life and, thus,
written this book.*

Heaven comes down to touch us
when we find ourselves safe in
the heart of another person.

Sharing

Thank you, my friend, for your arm flung around my shoulder in a moment of comradery, for half your tuna sandwich when I didn't have time to make lunch and for the loan of your car when mine wouldn't run. Thanks for getting half wet so I could stay half dry under your umbrella. Thanks for holding my hand as we pray, for hugging me while we cry and for laughing with me at the comedy of life. Thanks for the souvenir from your trip that means you thought of me while you were away. Thanks for sharing so much of yourself with me.

Selfless Love

Friendship. There's something so special about that word.

The world bows to people who have so committed themselves to each other.

In honor of friendship wars have been fought and won, fortunes have been given away, crowns have been relinquished.

In service to friendship we stand vigil at the bedside of the dying, adopt orphans, care for widows and clothe the needy. Friendship brings warmth to a shivering beggar, company to the lonely and laughter to the hurting.

In commitment to friendship men and women have been burned at the stake, torn apart by lions, maimed, imprisoned and martyred.

In tribute to friendship symphonies have been composed, classics written and masterpieces painted.

It is a word of respect and awe, a word of prayer and hope. It is love in its rarest, most selfless form . . . friendship.

Bridge

Friendship is the bridge between lonely and loved, between a glance and a gaze. It stretches from the fog into the sunshine, from hopelessness into faith. Friendship spans the gulf between despair and joy, between girl and boy. It crosses the chasm from hell to heaven, from God to man and from you to me.

Reflection

When we first met, you smiled warmly. It was a welcome and polite smile that extended friendship, and I knew I wanted to see it again. Time and togetherness spread that beautiful smile into your eyes, and they would twinkle happily when you saw me. Now, when I catch your eye, I can tell we have come to know each other very well. Your whole face lights up in sweet recognition. But I'm sure the light in your face is only a reflection of the smile on mine at that same moment.

Bits and Pieces

Bits and pieces.
Bits and pieces.
People. People important to you.
People unimportant to you cross your
life, touch it with love and move on.
There are people who leave you, and you
breathe a sigh of relief and wonder why
you ever came in contact with them.
There are people who leave you, and you
breathe a sigh of remorse and wonder
why they had to go and leave such a
gaping hole.

Children leave parents. Friends
leave friends. Acquaintances move on.
People change homes. People grow
apart. Enemies hate and move on.
Friends love and move on. You think of
the many who have moved into your hazy
memory. You look at those present and
wonder.

I believe in God's master plan in
lives. He moves people in and out of each
other's lives, and each leaves his mark on
the other. You find you are made up of
bits and pieces of all who ever touched
your life, and you are more because of it,
and you would be less if they had not
touched you.

Pray God that you accept the bits
and pieces in humility, and wonder, and
never question, and never regret.

Bits and pieces.

Bits and pieces.

— UNKNOWN

Enthusiasm

Enthusiasm! It's the thrill of living life to the max. It's the highest peak in life's roller coaster ride—that point when you squeal with delight, and your stomach jumps up into your throat. It's the swish of skis on powdery snow, glistening bows on surprise packages and the excited voice of your best friend.

Enthusiasm is the piccolo's trill in the "Star Spangled Banner." It's the snaggle-toothed grin of a little boy holding a triple-dip ice cream cone. It's the standing ovation for the winner in the Special Olympics. Yes, it's the up side of life and the anticipation of things to come. And it's how our friendship makes me feel.

Forgiveness

Forgiveness is not something we
need, you and I, for I have accepted you
as you are, and you me. You know that I
am weak and make mistakes. I disap-
point and hurt you, no doubt. But at the
same instant you know it is without inten-
tion or malice. And I know the same of
you. Because we have decided to be
friends, we simply forgave each other
once for all time—at the beginning.

Sticking Together

Together we stick;
divided we're stuck.

— EVON HEDLEY

I have decided to stick with love.
Hate is too great a burden to bear.

— MARTIN LUTHER KING, JR.

I don't know what
all this fuss is about.
In the first place,
you're not white; you're beige.
And I'm not black; I'm brown.
In our hearts we are the same.
So, you see, we're closer
than we think we are.

— UNKNOWN

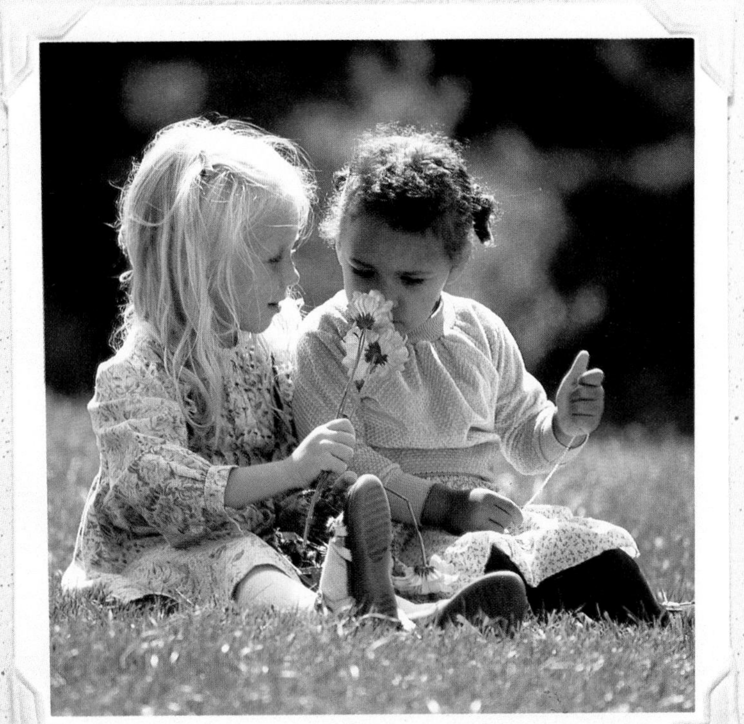

Congeniality

The pleasure of your company is a many-sided affair. It includes the pleasure of seeing you, the pleasure of hearing you talk, the drama of watching your actions, your likes and dislikes and adventures; the pleasure of hunting you up in your haunts, and the delicate flattery I feel when you hunt me up in mine. I mean all this and more when I say that I find you congenial. Congeniality, when once established between two kindred spirits or in a group, is the most carefree of human relationships. It is effortless, like purring. It is a basic theme in friendship.

— FRANCES LESTER WARNER (Adapted)

Eloquent Silence

We don't always have to talk, and I'm glad we're comfortable being quiet together. I draw incredible strength and hope by just being in the same room with you or walking with you through a quiet park. The silence between us says so many things eloquently. It says, "I trust you to understand my mood today." "I'm thankful I don't need to try and impress you with my words." "I love you, and you know it without my always having to say so." "I need to be with you today—just be with you."

If you must say something to me today, say it with a smile, a hug or a squeeze of my hand. I'll understand. Some things are better said with silence than with clumsy conversation. Let our silence continue.

A Lot Like Me

I like myself—I really do. Oh, it's not false pride as much as realizing that usually I'm all I've got. So, I'd rather be with someone I like for the rest of my life than with someone I don't.

Sure, I could be extremely hard on myself because I know my own faults better than anyone else. But the truth is, I'm doing the best I know how with all my heart, and I know it, whether anyone else can tell or not.

I love life and people and my work. And I've struggled hard through the years to be good at what I do. Oh, I know I haven't arrived yet, but I appreciate myself for who I am striving to become.

Sometimes I laugh with myself at myself, and sometimes we cry together. I have to take myself with a grain of salt (and a spoonful of sugar) and hope others will be gracious enough to take me that way, too. I give myself the benefit of the doubt and examine carefully my intent and effort, rather than my actual success or failure, for life is the striving, not just the accomplishment.

Yes, I like me — I admit it. I'm my own best friend. And because I like and accept myself for who and what I am, I can like and accept you as you are. Perhaps that's why I like you so much after all . . . you're a lot like me.

Because you bring me
nearer to God,
you are my friend.

— UNKNOWN

Comfortably Together

My coat and I live comfortably together. It has assumed all my wrinkles, does not hurt me anywhere, has molded itself to my deformities and is complacent to all my movements. I only feel its presence because it keeps me warm. Old coats and old friends are the same.

—VICTOR HUGO

Today

Our friendship cannot rely on our past together. And it cannot rely on the future we anticipate. It must be now. It must be today. For our past is only precious memories, and our future is still misty imaginings. Can't we find time to be together today?

Life is a series of surprises and would not be worth taking or keeping if it were not. God delights to isolate us every day and hide from us the past and the future.

—EMERSON

Changes

I don't mean to cling to you, my friend. It's just that I've had special friends before. We went along complacently assuming that life would remain the same and we would be together forever. Then one day they were gone, and I haven't been the same since. They left such an empty place in my life.

When I come too close to you it's because I'm afraid. It's because I know that we won't always be together. Life changes. People change. We will change. And, like most people, I'm afraid of change.

It's not that I want to possess you. I cherish our mutual freedom. It's just that I know our time together is probably limited, in one way or another, and I want to make the most of it while we can.

I like things the way they are between us—friends. Nothing more or less. So, if I come too close, let me know. I will try to back away. Or if, by chance, I begin to drift away from you, reach out and draw me back. Don't let our friendship change, except to deepen and grow.

Joy

The art of joy is having a love affair with life.

It is embracing life, drawing close to you all the beauty and wonder and goodness of the universe.

It is having a heart aglow with warmth for all your companions on the journey of life.

It is an expression of inner music. It is radiating joy as does a band of musicians marching down the street.

It is a blend of laughter and tears. Often it is the deep joy that comes to you through the mist of the years as you recall tender memories of joyous days gone by.

It is sharing your joy. "Some people," wrote the poet Walt Whitman, "are so much sunshine to the square inch." The joyous person seems to be plugged in to the sun itself.

It is celebrating life. The Master turned water into wine that the joyous wedding feast might continue. "Be of good cheer," he said. He proclaimed the purpose of his message to men in these words: "That my joy might be full."

It is the putting forth of all your powers. It is the flood-tide of inspiration, the glory of creation. As you work with joy you find joy in your work.

It is looking for the joys that come in small, precious packages and making the most of them, knowing that big packages of joy are few and far between.

It is making the most of now, enjoying what is at hand. It is taking time to enjoy life as you go along.

It is an awareness of the heaven that exists all about you. As Solomon said: "He that hath a bountiful eye shall be blessed." It is making each day your most wonderful day.

Joy is the flag you fly when the Prince of Peace is in residence within your heart.

Joy is love bubbling forth into life.

—WILFERD A. PETERSON

Togetherness

I was the weekend guest of a couple
in their mid-sixties who lived a solitary
country life, depended mainly on each
other for company, and still conversed
together with the interest and animation
of old friends catching up after a long
absence. When I remarked on this, my
host said, "To feel really close to another
person one must keep a little distance."
In other words, we must avoid the aggres-
sive shaping of one person by the other.
How seldom we are aware of the tremen-
dous pressure we put on our families and
friends to be as we want them to be,
rather than the unique persons they are.
The basic message of human communi-
cation is, "Here I am; there you are. We
are not alone."

—JOHN K. LAGEMANN

The Windy Auburn Hair

My sweet friend with the windy
auburn hair. I don't see her every day,
even though we'd both like that. When
I do, she comes to me with a song to sing
or a tale to tell. We sing and laugh, and
then she's gone. She has things to do.
I do, too. And the days she cannot come
are long, watching and wishing for my
sweet friend with the windy auburn hair.

Solitude

Solitude is creativity's dearest friend.
She allows creativity total freedom to be
whatever she must be. Creative ideas
chase each other happily through solitude's park, playing hide-'n-seek, each
one secretly hoping to be caught and
tamed. Other times, creativity curls up in
the big, soft easy chair before the warm
fire of solitude. And together they dream
and doze and dream again. Solitude
gently encourages her friend to give the
most of herself, to be the best at what she
attempts. And creativity responds with a
sonnet, a symphony, a masterpiece or a
proverb. Rich friendship such as this is
born of time—quiet, comfortable hours
together dreaming and sharing.

Empathy

Empathy is your hurt in my heart. It is your unspoken pain flowing as tears from my eyes. It is my feeling of melancholy today because of your sorrow. And it's that nervous, queasy feeling in the pit of my stomach because you're facing a difficult task.

But empathy is also the song I sing when you're happy. It's the exhilaration and pride I know when you get a standing ovation. It's your joy expressing itself in my laughter. And it's your peace that calms my heart.

Empathy is your soul living in me.

*Friendship is
the marriage of the soul.*

—Voltaire

Friend of Friends

He is the King of kings, the Lord of lords. And He is the Friend of friends. Out of His magnificent power and glory Jesus gently kissed away the tears of the heavy-hearted. He reached out in kindness to touch and tenderly heal the hurting.

He gave the gift of life to a weeping mother and taught His followers a better way to live. He let the loved disciple rest his weary head on His heart. He was their Friend, with all its richest meanings. He met their needs and allowed them to meet His. He was the Friend of friends. He loved. "Greater love hath no man than this, that He should lay down His life for His friends."

So I asked,
"Lord, how much do you love me?"
He smiled and answered,
"I love you this much."
Then he stretched out his arms
and died.

—UNKNOWN

Apology

I know you've probably already forgiven me, but I want to apologize to you anyway, my friend. I'm sure I owe you more than one apology for some pain I have caused you unaware. I know I have hurt you with an unthinking word I have spoken, an unintended insult that slashed at your heart or a casual remark that brought a tear to your eye. How incredible that I could treat you so and, yet, you still choose to call me your friend.

Please accept this apology for the one I failed to make at the moment it was needed. Or save it for that moment when I will not know that I have hurt you, for I would never have it so. I apologize, my friend, because our relationship is precious to me—far more precious than pride or pretense. As the old song so aptly says, "We always hurt the ones we love." I'm sorry.

Friendtuition

Even from across the room I can tell by the pitch of your voice whether you're happy or bored. And the slope of your shoulders says you're discouraged or exhilarated. Your hands let me know if you're nervous or calm. And I can see behind your eyes to your inner joy or pain. Your swinging foot says you are frustrated. And the way you play with your ring helps me guess your preoccupation. Some days you laugh and talk excitedly, but other days you're quiet, tired and pensive.

The mystery of friendship is that two people, though separated by distance, can be so close. It's a kind of friendtuition, I believe. The sadness of it all is that two people might sit side by side and yet remain miles apart.

Free to Be Friends

Peace and joy bless the friend
who comes to see and hear
and not to change.

At the heart of love
there is a simple secret:
the lover lets the beloved be free.

—UNKNOWN

*Thank you for loving me
with your arms open.*

*No one worth possessing
can be quite possessed.*

—SARAH TEASDALE

Knowing You, Knowing Me

You understand what I have left unsaid. You appreciate in me things I have long since taken for granted. You suggest the improvements I need to make for areas of my life I had written off as hopeless. And you challenge me to use talents I deny or help me see when I'm chasing pipe dreams. You call me to higher aspirations than I can imagine for myself and give me courage to try new things. In knowing you, I no longer wonder who I really am because, through you, I see my own dignity, honor and worth. Through you I am able to overcome my feelings of failure and weakness. In you I see a clearer image of me. In knowing you, I know me.

Meeting you was like suddenly seeing myself in a mirror.

We were never strangers you and I— only friends yet unfound.

—UNKNOWN

Friends of the Heart

I don't want to be just another friend that tugs away at you for your precious time, your attention and your love. I want to be someone you come to for understanding, someone to whom you retreat for emotional rest. I want to be someone with whom you can laugh and share your joy, one on whose shoulder you can cry without embarrassment or apology and one whose hand you can reach for when you need comfort or support. I want you to be able to say to me, "I feel lonely today; stay with me a while longer." Or, "Can you come over? I need to talk to you." I just want to be there for you, as you so often are for me. I want us to be friends of the heart.

Expectations

If you expect perfection from people, your whole life is a series of disappointments, grumblings and complaints. If, on the contrary, you pitch your expectations low, taking folks as the inefficient creatures they are, you are frequently surprised by having them perform better than you had hoped.

—BRUCE BARTON

Come Again Soon

Your letter came today amidst magazines, circulars and bills, and my heart tripped over itself in anticipation. I purposely tucked it on the bottom of the stack, saving the best for last. When finally I came to the happy yellow envelope, I paused. I went to the kitchen and fixed myself a cup of tea, then curled up in my favorite chair on the sun porch to savor every word.

It was almost like having you there with me, for we had sat talking on that porch so often before you moved away. I could hear your voice and see your laughing brown eyes. You teased me gently as always and counseled me with your quiet wisdom. You bared your troubled soul and shared your joyful heart.

So, it was with a sigh of contentment and a sense of remorse that I came to the familiar "I love you" at the end. I sat quietly for several minutes, sipping my tea, remembering . . . wishing. Please come again soon. I miss you.